LETTERS

To my mom

IN HEAVEN

THIS BOOK BELONGS TO:

....

....

DATE _____

DATE _____

DATE _____

DATE _____

DATE _____

DATE _____

DATE _____

DATE _____

DATE _____

DATE _____

DATE _____

DATE _____

DATE _____

DATE _____

DATE _____

DATE _____

DATE _____

DATE _____

DATE _____

DATE _____

DATE _____

DATE _____

DATE _____

DATE _____

DATE _____

DATE _____

DATE _____

DATE _____

DATE _____

DATE _____

DATE _____

DATE _____

DATE _____

DATE _____

DATE _____

DATE _____

DATE _____

DATE _____

DATE _____

DATE _____

DATE _____

DATE _____

DATE _____

DATE _____

DATE _____

DATE _____

DATE _____

DATE _____

DATE _____

DATE _____

DATE _____

DATE _____

DATE _____

DATE _____

DATE _____

DATE _____

DATE _____

DATE _____

DATE _____

DATE _____

DATE _____

DATE _____

DATE _____

DATE _____

DATE _____

DATE _____

DATE _____

DATE _____

DATE _____

DATE _____

DATE _____

DATE _____

DATE _____

DATE _____

DATE _____

DATE _____

DATE _____

DATE _____

DATE _____

DATE _____

DATE _____

DATE _____

DATE _____

DATE _____

DATE _____

DATE _____

DATE _____

DATE _____

Made in United States
North Haven, CT
27 February 2024

49321602R00055